Created to Stand Out

Not Fit In

Sherique Dill

Scripture quotations marked KJV are from the King James Version. Scripture quotations marked NKJV are from the New King James Version.

Special discounts are available on quantity purchases by corporations, associations, and others. For details, contact the author at the address above.

Table of Contents

Dedication

I dedicate this book to my wonderful children Joden, Jyelle, and Jendayia Dill. I'm happy to be your mother. My objective is always to leave a family legacy that you can be proud of. I know that you'll be proud to have me as your mother.

To all the readers and people that follow my work- I appreciate you. My work would be nothing without you. I wrote this book in confidence, not knowing what support I would get, and throughout the years, you've supported me.

To all the unique people in the world. Those not willing to conform and fit in. 'Created to Stand Out Not Fit In', is for you!

Introduction

Technology is a force to reckon with. It is a force that has grown and continues to grow rapidly. This new era is quickly erasing the world we once knew. Righteous standards, morals, values, and beliefs are being replaced by what they now call the 'new normal'. The things once considered abnormal are normal. The world seeks to redefine what is natural and unnatural.

However, the systems of this world aren't solely responsible for the evil we see happening daily. One of our major abilities is to choose. We have the power to make our own decisions. We are the masters of our destiny. Many people have decided to follow certain practices and agendas that are against natural principles and standards. They submit to the wicked will of others; just to be accepted.

Consciously or unconsciously many people are attracted to these types of things, and they trade their beliefs, values, morals, and standards to avoid being persecuted. If you are a conformist and you are void of your own identity, you will become spiritually and emotionally extinct; someone else or something else will be in control of your life. People that embrace what makes them unique, practice self-love, and appreciate themselves, live very enjoyable lives. They are the people who engage in the things that make them happy and pursue the things that they are passionate about. These are the people that contribute to the betterment of humanity. Their goal is to be of service. They are not selfish. They stand out from the crowd and are easily identified. Their energy is so electrifying that when you're in the presence of them, great things happen.

The world is working towards conformity, humanism, and a one-world order. Don't forget the foundation on which everything is built: knowing who you are, why you are, and for what purpose.

It's very easy to lose your identity in this 'new society'. Family, friends, associates, and even your favorite celebrity seek to control your mind and keep you in an illusion. Distracting you from knowing who you are and why you are. You must act like light and salt. Light does not conform to darkness nor does it blend in. Salt also does not blend in when you use it; salt is dominant. Salt prevents decay. It can be used to preserve things. Like salt, we preserve the natural principles, laws, and concepts of The Universe. There are four agents of change (Light, salt, yeast, seed). Yeast is used for expansion. Whatever organization we're a part of, and whatever we do, the ending results should be better than how we found it. This is expansion. Seeds represent growth, and whatever we sow we shall reap.

Conformity means to yield or adjust to the thoughts, behaviors, and pressures of others to fit in or to be accepted and approved. Here is a simple example of conformity. Your best friend loves to watch horror movies. You don't particularly like horror. To please your best friend, and you don't want to seem boring, or uncooperative, you subject yourself to your friend's will, and make yourself unpleasant, to avoid rejection. Conformity terminates uniqueness. When uniqueness is not present you lose your originality. You lose your dignity and respect. It is your responsibility to make people respect you for who you are, not what they wish you to be. This is the height of self-value and self-worth.

IT SEEMS AS IF EVERYONE is competing with one another, but the truth is; if you follow your life's purpose you will have no competition. Trying to compete with others is a disservice to self. It is also ignorance because we must understand that each of us was given a divine calling from The Most High working together for the betterment of humanity.

If you function within your calling, you can rise above the spirit of imitation. This book encourages people to embrace their uniqueness, to see themselves the way The Most High sees them, to love and appreciate themselves, to adhere to their code of conduct, and to never compromise to be accepted by others. This book is intended to uplift the mind and to display that if you change the way you think about yourself there will be no limits to your success. Our potentials are limitless.

You must be bold, confident, courageous, unshakable, and unwavering. This doesn't mean that you can't study successful people and learn strategies from them. I am a huge proponent of mentorship. If there is a person who is successful in what you wish to do, you can study their steps, or observe them. This is good to do because you want to achieve the same results. However, you must be a student and not a follower. The difference between a student and a follower is that a student listens and determines for themselves what they will do. They make their own decisions. A follower listens and does whatever the leader or mentor says, without questioning their logic. They feel as if something is wrong, but they trust the leader or mentor's logic more than they trust themselves. If a leader says that the sky is red, a follower doesn't verify this information, they just believe it. A student will look up and see that the sky is blue.

All of the topics that are included in Created to Stand Out Not Fit In, make you stand out. When you follow these principles, you feel a higher level of self-love. You accept all of your faults and realize that they make you who you are. You won't crave the opinion of others when it comes to you but rather rely on your strength. Created to Stand Out's objective is to boost your self-motivation, so that you can rely on your greatest asset: you.

Chapter One
Be Driven by Purpose

———

Before you can begin to understand your life's purpose you must accept yourself for who you are. You must begin to accept yourself the way the Creator sees you. Do you know that you are a Co-Creator with God? You are divine, and you have creative energy. You have the same ability to create as The Most High creates so that you can serve your function in the world. For example, when God said "Let there be light'" there was light. When you say, "I am powerful, I am blessed, I am creative and intelligent," the same principle applies. You can create your reality.

When you lack purpose, you become confused and have no sense of direction. Confusion sends you in any direction, and most times the direction will be one that you dread. I remember living day after day not knowing what my purpose was. I was not exposed to the concept of purpose until I read a book by Dr. Myles Munroe called 'Unleash Your Purpose'. After reading this book I understood why I felt as if something was missing. There was a great void in my life and I needed it to be filled. I needed to get more involved in making a difference in the lives of others, and I needed to feel as if I was making greater contributions to humanity. My life has never been the same after discovering that God made me for a specific purpose and that there are some things that only I could do.

<u>What is your life's purpose?</u>

Your life's purpose is simply your reason for existing. I like to call it my mission because I am a diplomat on Earth with a special assignment from The Most High. I am a special agent of The Creator. I am an agent of change. I believe that when I was a spirit in the heavenly realm, I either chose my destiny or it was chosen for me by The Most High. Either way, I accepted it, and this is why when I engage in these things, I feel good because my spirit knows that I'm on the right track. When you're off track, you'll feel it within your spirit. You will feel like something is missing and you will feel a sense of restlessness. This is a sign that you're trying to find your correct path.

Your purpose is not for you. Your purpose is much bigger than you. Your ancestors and your generation are relying on the completion of your mission/purpose. When you expire, will you be received into the celestial realms with honor, or will you be shunned away? Don't be distracted by the things of this world, to the point where you lose your way and you ignore the mission. You can never function properly if you do not understand why you even exist. Everything starts and ends with a purpose.

The Creator and You know your Purpose

When you have a relationship with the Universe/Creator, recognizing what your life's mission is would flow effortlessly. Furthermore, being more in tune with yourself, and who you are will also help you with this. Many people cannot determine why they exist, or what their true passion is because they don't pay attention to their thoughts and feelings. They are not in alignment with their divine trinity: body, soul, and spirit.

Here are four important steps:

1. Awareness of self
2. Acceptance of self
3. Acknowledgment of self
4. Action

Even though I was aware that I had a special purpose, like many, I wasn't exactly clear on what I should be doing. Every day I declared that I was living my purpose and constantly prayed for revelations and spiritual insight. No one was able to help me with this. People can give you information that can help guide you, but you must put in the work and recognize your destiny. Others could only assume or guess what it is.

The Manufacturer Knows Everything There is to Know About the Product

I believe in a higher power. I think we should be able to agree that we didn't create ourselves. We didn't place the sun in the sky, or place the beautiful seas where they are. All we know is that nature exists. Something had to be responsible for the creation of all things.

When you go into a store to buy a toaster, all you see is the finished product. You have no idea of the time that was put into constructing this toaster, the materials that were needed, the mechanical wiring, and how many times it had to be tested to ensure it was working properly.

Before the manufacturer made the toaster he/she knew exactly what the purpose and the potential of his/her product would be. The toaster was made to fulfill the needs of the manufacturer. You, the consumer, don't know all the specific details of the toaster. You know the color of it, you can describe what it looks like, and you have an idea of what problems the item can solve. You get the full information when you read the manual or the instructions. The manual is attached to the product and is provided by the manufacturer (the one who knows everything about the product).

If for any reason the manufacturer decides not to give you a manual, you would have no idea how to use the toaster. You would never know how to fully maximize the potential of the toaster or what not to do to damage it. For example, you can destroy the toaster by emerging it into the water because you were not aware that it should not emerge into the water. It is ignorant to operate things without information.

You will perish for living in ignorance. Ignorance is an enemy to the purpose of a thing. This is why you must always read the instructions before using any product. This protects you from damages and possible health risks. When you decide to operate something that you have no information on, you instantly take away value from the product. Why have a toaster and not know all the benefits of the toaster? The best consumer is a knowledgeable consumer. Also, when you maximize the purpose of why the toaster was made, you will love the toaster even more.

This is how it is with the Creator. The Universe/Creator is the manufacturer and you are the product. When you seek to communicate with the Creator the manual for your life will flow through your heart or your spirit.

Some Ways You Communicate With the Creator

You can communicate with the Creator through:

A. Prayer
B. Worship, Singing
C. Breathing and Meditation
D. Being in nature (sunlight, beaches, gardens, parks, etc.)

Being Addicted to Your Purpose

To be 'addicted' is to be devoted or loyal to a practice or habit. This is a true passion. To engage in something that you can't pull yourself from. Many people are addicted to dangerous or bad habits such as drinking alcohol, smoking, being lazy, not being loyal to schedules, promiscuity, dishonesty, and more. If you can apply the same principle with good habits, success is bound to be yours. You should feel empty when you don't get to do the things that you love. If a day goes by and you have not done anything that you are passionate about you should feel as if your day was wasted. When you wake up in the morning the first thing that should be on your mind is your purpose. You should have a clear plan for what you will do. The last thing you think about before you go to bed should be your life's purpose. Your purpose should be so magnetic that you just can't seem to pull yourself away from it. When night comes you should only go to sleep because your body needs to rest, but you're always eager and excited to see where your life's mission will take you, and what gifts it will bring you. Program your mind to believe that you can't live without your purpose and that if you can't do what the Creator created you to do, your existence is useless.

Every morning you wake up, let purpose be on your mind. When you go to bed at night, the purpose should be on your mind. My addiction to purpose was so strong that I got frustrated if I could not work towards fulfilling it. It fulfilled me and every time I tried to withdraw myself away from it, I suffered from withdrawal symptoms. My mission is my life's line, it is my spiritual umbilical cord. Knowing and acting on your purpose makes you stand out from the crowd.

If something was created without a reason, it has no business existing at all. I am an addict for 'purpose'. It gives me true meaning and inspiration. Time is never wasted when purpose consumes it.

Chapter Two
Gifts and Abilities

———

We have already established that The Most High has created us for a purpose. It's important to understand that to complete your purpose effectively, you must utilize your gifts (divine abilities). You have been equipped with these gifts. They are natural and inept. The Creator would not create you for a purpose without giving you the proper tools to be successful. All of us were blessed with gifts and special abilities. However, people are so busy imitating others that they are never discovered. When you use your gifts, you will stand out from the crowd. When you operate in your gifted realm, people will flock to you because they need what you have. People that use their gifts aren't ordinary beings. They are extraordinary.

The journey was not over for me when I became aware of my purpose. I then had to contemplate the things that I enjoyed doing. Not only did I focus on the things that I enjoyed, but I had to find the things that I was deeply passionate about. I had to be careful of 'like'. I understood that not because I 'liked' a particular thing meant that I was called to do it. I didn't want to get caught up in doing the things that only satisfied me but caught up in doing things I was assigned to do.

You can always learn how to do things by practice and study. But, gifts are often natural and they don't require much hard work. Gifts are God-given abilities that you perform so well that people describe them as being 'blessed' by God. Your gifts are your area of influence. You will know it's a gift because people will continuously be amazed by it. Some people need some help with a gift that they have because they haven't recognized the potential of that gift. So, they have a mentor to guide them and help them to maximize the potential of that gift. For example, I didn't recognize that I was a gifted inspirational writer and coach. I started my writing journey when a friend spoke to me about writing and how I should write too. The gift was there, hidden like a treasure, but it was exposed through this friend. I always expressed myself extraordinarily well through writing, and I always had a great ability to say things that inspired others. But I didn't see it as a gift. Eventually, I realized my inspirational and self-help gifts. It was in my genes, however, it took time to be discovered. The Universe will always give you what you need, to get you where you need to be. Furthermore, the Universe will always connect you with the right people to help you be what you were created to be.

Being You is Effortless

No one else can execute a thing the way you can. Even though people try to mimic your gift or talent, always remember that they will never do it as smoothly as you. The reason is that God gave the gift to you and not to them. It's a part of individuality. None of us are alike. There are natural gifts hidden inside all of us. Sometimes you may feel as if you do not have any natural gifts or that there is nothing you are outstanding in. You have to search deeper within yourself. Something special is there that you might not be aware of. Go back into your childhood if you need to. Try to remember the things that made you happy and the things you did effortlessly. You will soon realize that you are more gifted in one area than another. These are the things you should be focused on.

Gifts and Abilities are not the Same

There is a difference between being skilled in an area and having a gift. People today seem not to understand that a gift is much deeper than being skillful. Your gifts are your superpower. They are the things that you'll be known for. When you operate in your gifted area, when people have a particular problem they think of you. If no one thinks of you when they have a particular problem, then you haven't discovered the power of your gift as yet. You must discover the power of your gift and put it before the world.

Many gifts can be inherited from one's bloodline or generation such as parents, grandparents, or even great-grandparents. If you trace back within your family line, you will often find the same gifts. For example, if one member of a family is a musician, let's say the mother, most likely the daughter, son, or grandchild has the musical gene. It was passed to you through cellular memory. Gifts are given by God and chosen by you. What does this mean? You came to Earth to solve a particular problem, however, you must choose it. You must accept your destiny. Some people don't accept their destiny, they hide their potential.

In your personal life, separate your skills from your gifts so that they can be clear. On a sheet of paper, draw two columns. Write down your skills on one side, and write down the things that you think you're best at. The things that you perform effortlessly.

These are most likely your gifts. Now go out into the world and own them. I dare you to be different!

Skills and Abilities are Developed and Expected

Skills are usually learned and developed by others. Skills are things such as excellent customer service, good communication, typing, technical abilities, teaching, multi-tasking, athletics, etc. People learn them to be valuable in the marketplace or the business world. You're not naturally good at them. It took lots of hard work, study and practice to excel in the skill. Enhancing your skills requires years of practice. Most professional athletes undergo extensive training to be the world-class athletes that they are. The results of skills and abilities are expected and calculated. Also, you don't feel fulfilled by the skill, it's just a job or way for you to make money. If you're attending guitar classes, you expect to be able to play the guitar. If you go to college to learn business administration, you expect to be a professional in this field. However, it is quite different with gifts.

Gifts are Matured and Surprising

God-given abilities (gifts) are things such as leadership, inspirational speaking, creativity, being artistic, singing, and others. Gifts mature and become more powerful as you use them. They give you a different feeling. They give you a sense of fulfillment and happiness. Whatever you're gifted in, you make it a part of your lifestyle. While with skills and abilities, you can change them as you wish and do different things. Also, you can retire from performing certain skills and abilities, but you never retire from your true work (gifts).

When you use your gifts, you can expect the unexpected because you're operating in a realm where possibilities are endless. The Universe is open to you and many times you will be surprised and overwhelmed. There will be many times because of your gifts, you discover more things you are great at. Sometimes you may feel discouraged and disappointed, and out of nowhere, an opportunity arises that takes you before great men and women. This is the power of operating in your true self. When you operate out of your true self, you will find yourself encountering many obstacles and challenges with no breakthrough. Everything you seem to do doesn't work for you or bring you success. Find your true self, and success will be attracted to you.

Gifts are to be Used to Serve Humanity

When you go to college or a learning institution to learn a skill, you can use that skill in the marketplace to obtain the money you need to take care of your needs and wants. In the marketplace, you will be compensated based on the value of your skills and abilities. If your skills are valuable you get paid more, if they are not as valuable, you get paid less.

However, with gifts, you use them to serve humanity. Your God-given abilities should be used as your contribution to the world. It should be more than for monetary gain. I'm not saying that you shouldn't be paid for using your gifts, but that should not be the basis of why you use them. When you can perform in a certain area for free, even if you're not paid to do it, this is how you know it is your calling or ministry. You're not thinking about yourself and how it benefits you, but rather how it benefits others. It makes you feel more meaningful because you're making a big impact on the world. When you die, what will other people say about you? Will they be able to testify on how you've helped them? Will the life that you've lived reflect a person who dedicated their time and effort to the progress of society? Now is the time to work on your legacy and how you want to be remembered when you depart Earth. This is what it means to stand out and not fit in. Many people only care about themselves and their families. They don't care about other people and their struggles. Use the gifts given to you by the Creator to serve humanity and make the world a better place.

Chapter Three
Avoiding Idleness

The spirit of idleness is deceitful. You should avoid being idle because it's like a parasite. Being idle will keep you far away from fulfilling your life's purpose. Idleness chases success. If you hang around people that have no vision or goals, they have a mandate. Their mandate is to convert you. You will do the same things that they do, and be unsuccessful just like them. The people that love idleness will never produce anything worth living for because idleness hinders productivity. When you become spiritually mature you see life differently. People that stand out from the crowd don't have time to waste doing nothing. They are ambitious and goal achievers.

Busy People are not Always Productive

Standing out from the crowd means maximizing your time and being productive. This is very important because some people are always busy. But, they're busy doing things that don't matter or don't have a positive impact on their lives. Some people are busy gossiping, watching television all day, partying, and engaging in social media. If you ask them what they did to become one step closer to achieving a goal, they can't tell you. Time is being consumed. Time can never be recovered. Some people spend 80% of their time doing irrelevant things, and 20% on things that are. What major shift could happen in their lives if this was switched around? What if people could use 80% of their time doing things that are meaningful and productive? Think of all the things you could accomplish and how you could spiral into a wave of achievements.

I had to stand out and be different. I refused to get involved with people or spend time in conversations that would not positively impact me. I was now living a life of purpose and time was precious. The older I became the more valuable my time manifested. I started to set more goals and prepare more plans for my life. The moment I decided to be disciplined I noticed progress. As I reflected on life, it was clear that being disciplined and setting goals makes a big difference. Walk away from people that don't encourage you to invest your time but consume it.

There is a Time and Place for Recreation

Recreation and enjoyment of life are very important. It's not wise to not have a good balance. This can cause a false sense of happiness, where you achieve a lot but you're not happy because you're not enjoying life. So always include creative things in your schedule that you can enjoy. When you achieve your goals, treat yourself.

Some people go overboard with entertainment. They don't achieve anything worthwhile because of their luxurious lifestyle. The money that should be used to achieve goals, is being spent on dining, partying, and a lavish lifestyle. When you use your money to buy things that bring you a return, it is an asset. When you spend money on things that don't bring you a return, it's a liability.

So, realize that there is a time and place for everything. There is a time to laugh and enjoy life, and a time for business. While you are in your youth, you should be setting up a good life for yourself and your family. Sow your seeds while you're young and vibrant so that you can reap the harvest as you get older. This means that there is no time for idleness and being unproductive.

Gossiping

According to the Merriam-Webster dictionary, 'Gossip' means "To indulge in idle talk or rumors about others; spreading of sensational stories."

Gossipers want to take the attention off themselves and direct it towards others. When they can shed light on other people's faults, it makes them feel good. They don't want other people to recognize their imperfections. They believe that if they can distract their friends and family with gossip, these friends and family members won't have the time and energy to look deeper into their lives and criticize them. They use the imperfection of others to hide their truth. The time you take to gossip and worry about other people's lives can be used for your healing and restoration. These are the cowards. They recognize that they have challenges that need to be addressed, but they look for things to distract them. Gossiping is a distraction. It eats up all of your productive time and prolongs your healing.

Gossiping is a Time Killer

Think about all of the things you could have done instead of being on the phone with your friend having small talks. What plan could you have developed for your life? Whatever you put into the Universe it will come back to you. Standing out from the crowd requires you to watch the words that come out of your mouth. You should always seek to speak positive words. Gossiping causes you to get involved in conversations that are often negative. When you speak badly about others, you close the doors for divine opportunities to flow in your life. Always have the attitude of a diplomat. You're a servant of the Most High.

Idle talking can also get you into a lot of trouble. It causes great disappointment. Some people may feel as if their idle talking is fellowship, but it is not fellowship if your conversation is not positive or uplifting to another. Now, don't get me wrong, there is nothing wrong with socializing and getting involved in good debatable conversations. A conversation that will introduce a solution to a problem, inspire others, or help you to gain knowledge is good. When the conversation changes and brings up someone else's name and talks about them in a less favorable way it is time to exit the conversation. If you are not learning anything positive in a conversation, exit.

Your Idea is not for Everyone to Know

Idleness causes you to reveal your ideas or goals to people that don't need to know. Some people would do anything within their power to see that you fail. Some people don't want you to become successful because they are not. So they aim to kill your dream or vision and to make sure it doesn't manifest. For example; when a woman is pregnant, there are rules that she should abide by if she wants to have a healthy baby. If she neglects these rules her unborn baby would be in jeopardy.

Napoleon Hill, from the book 'Think and Grow Rich" says, "Those who talk too much do little else. If you talk more than you listen, you not only deprive yourself of many opportunities to accumulate useful knowledge, but you also disclose your plans and purposes to people who will take great delight in defeating you because they envy you."

Wise People Keep a Still Tongue

It is good to keep a still tongue. Those who are always heard can be perceived as strong, bold, or brave. But, sometimes speaking too much can either show how wise you are, or how ignorant you are. Besides, how can you learn, if you are always talking? You shouldn't be talking too much when you are in the presence of wise people. You should be listening. If you are around people that have proven methods of success, this is a good opportunity to gain free knowledge. So a good, gentle, meek, and quiet spirit when in the presence of great people is required. People that talk too much are often rude and not considerate of other people's feelings. This is not bold, it is immature. Only children express themselves without care or concern. It takes maturity to express yourself in a way that is not offensive to others. We need to be careful not to burn our bridges. The people you insult might be the people you need later on in life. A brother or sister insulted is hard to reach.

Who Should You Talk To?

Discuss your goals and strategies with people that are supportive and inspiring. The only person that has to believe in your vision is you. So if you have a friend that doesn't understand your vision, that's okay. Once that friend supports you and will help you to get where you need to be, that's good. Support is more than just a good talk. So, look for people who can do more than just say, "Congratulations". These are the type of friends that always congratulate, you but never see the value in your work, to do more. For example, you talk to your friend about how you started a business, and they say to you, " That's great, congratulations. I wish you all the best." But, they never support you financially or in other ways.

You should interact with people that have the same mindset as you. If you are full of ideas and they are full of ideas, you have no reason to feel threatened. If you think of success and they think of success, both will achieve success. This is important because as humans we feed off of the energy of others. This is how we learn different things. Dr. Myles Munroe said, "If I am the smartest person in the group, it's time for me to find another group". If you're the smartest person in the group, people are being energized off of you, but how are you growing? It's vital to understand that if you're not growing you're dying. Your entourage should be filled with a variety of people with different gifts, and these gifts should be able to benefit you. This is what you call having a mastermind group. A group of people that can help each other. When you have a mastermind group you achieve more. You don't need to know everything. People are so infested with the 'diy'(do it yourself) mindset. Wise people capitalize on their strengths and hire their weaknesses. A good example of this is Henry Ford. Henry Ford didn't know how to do a lot of things, however, he looked for people that had the skills he needed. Together, they accomplished success.

Three Types of People That you should Consider Having in Your Life

Spiritual Mentor: Your holy trinity is the body, mind, and spirit. These three entities need each other. Spirituality is very important. Your spirit is the divine part of you, or the eternal part of you that is connected to The Most High (Creator). While the body and the mind perisheth, the spirit lives on forever. You must keep your spirit in tune, or you will find yourself 'fitting in' to please others.

In your mastermind group, have a spiritual mentor. Spiritual mentors help to keep you on your path and they help to keep you grounded in your faith or your belief system. Life comes with its uncertainties and we often need someone with spiritual values to encourage us.

Financial Mentor: Many people are not poor because they lack the means to money. Many people are poor because they lack financial literacy or financial support. They don't have good money management skills. People don't have good money management skills because they don't study people that do. As I said earlier, you don't need to know everything, however, this is one skill I would suggest you know for yourself. No one will ever be a better steward of your money, than you. Until you grow and develop better in finances, find a mentor that you can learn from. I follow Robert Kiyosaki, Peter Schiff, Jim Rickards, Dave Ramsay, Gregory Mannarino, and a host of other financial experts.

Some people say that money is the root of all evil. This is a misconception. What you do with the money that you have determines whether it is the root of all evil or the path to heaven on earth. When you have money in abundance you can help more people. Money makes good people better, and bad people worse. Evaluate your thoughts on money and stand out from the crowd!

A Comedian: This may sound strange to you but the pressures of life can get you down. It is good to have a friend that can bring laughter into your life. When things are going wrong they always know how to make you smile and release the pressure and stress from your life. This is so important. These types of friends will normally teach you to approach disappointments more calmly. Laughter reduces stress and you will live longer if you have it. Isn't it amazing how God gave us a sense of humor? These types of friends are very valuable; I don't care how rich you are, if you do not have laughter and a merry heart, your life will be worth living. You will not be able to enjoy true happiness.

Chapter Four
Being Unique and Original

There is no human being on this Earth with the same fingerprint as another. Each of us has a unique fingerprint. This means that we are unique. What makes us unique is our genetic makeup, our experiences, our thoughts and perceptions, and much more. This is why it is self-cruelty when you compare yourself to others. We grew up in different environments and experienced different things. When we experience things, we either perceive them as a threat or as something good. You should never be ashamed of who you are, and what you've become. Everything that happened to you, happened for a reason. The Most High allowed you to go through some things to strengthen your spiritual muscles.

Contemplate all of the things that you went through in your life. Would you be where you are now if you didn't go through these things? Would you have the incredible level of strength that you have now if it weren't for these experiences?

Definition of Unique

According to Merriam-Webster Dictionary, unique is defined as "Being the only one, being without a like or equal, distinctive, or unusual". This is exactly what you are, you have no equal.

You are Unique

Sometimes I felt like I just didn't fit in. Many organizations I wanted to join, but it didn't work out well for me because it would mean I had to give up my uniqueness and just be a follower. Some organizations don't allow you to be who you are or vocal about how you feel. Some leaders act as if they're all-powerful. However, leadership is a privilege. People don't have to follow if they don't want to, and who will you teach? I had to accept who I was. I realized that there was nothing wrong or weird about me. I am a leader. I am not a follower. I am a student. When I meet a mentor or teacher, I listen to them and determine for myself if what they're saying makes sense. If it makes sense and I feel good in my spirit about it, I incorporate it into my lifestyle. If I don't agree with it, I don't choose it. I make my own decisions. I don't allow people to make decisions for me. Followers don't make their own decisions. They trust the leader or teacher more than they trust themselves. If the leader tells them that the sky is red, they will believe it without asking questions or verifying this information. Even though it is easy to verify, they won't.

We are masters of our destiny. No human being is superior or greater than the next. All of us are co-creators with the Creator. How are we co-creators? By using two words: I am. Whatever comes after I am, you are. So, you shall have what you say. Isn't this creating?

So, to stand out from the crowd means to embrace what makes you unique. It means to become one with your divinity. You are a magnificent being operating in a physical body. You are a King or Queen. You must see yourself this way. You can see things with your mind's eye and bring them into manifestation. If you can dream it, you can create it!

We are unique and different. We are not sheep. If you are a person that believes that you exist to make a difference, you cannot just fit in. Wherever we go, our light must shine brighter. We must influence people with our positive attitude, productive mindset, morals and so much more. Could you imagine if all of us were alike? Wouldn't we operate like robots? That would take the fun and exuberance out of life. We all have one soul, which is the human soul. But our actions, behavior, experiences, skills, gifts, beliefs, and perceptions make us different. The difference is good.

Don't allow anyone to rob you of what makes you unique. There is something special about you that should be easily identified when you walk into the presence of people. For example, when I'm in the presence of people I inspire, I bring light, I lead, I influence, I am diplomatic, and a servant of the people. What are some things that make you unique when you are in the presence of people?

Things that Make You Unique

- **Character-** Your character is different from another person because a character is formed by your parents, environment, family, teachers, experiences, and beliefs. How you communicate with others displays your type of character. Your character traits can be tolerance, truthfulness, alertness, integrity, courage, and honesty. You might be a humble person, helpful, peaceful, resourceful, enthusiastic, or goal-oriented. These are some of the traits that people observe when they come in contact with you. This is how they determine what type of person you are. Your character is a brand. People that interact with you constantly will know the things you will do and what you will not do because of your character. No matter what type of parents you have, or what environment you came from, you can change your character if you don't like it. You can choose to be honest, loyal, humble, peaceful, and down to earth.

• **Beliefs-** Most of the things that you believe have been taught to you since you were a child. What you think about life, about yourself and your religious beliefs play a significant role because it will determine your code of conduct and standards. The things that you believe determine the decisions you make. Your belief system is very powerful because as a man or woman thinketh so is he or she. You are what you believe. Some beliefs exist from the lies that we've been taught by others. These beliefs limit and set boundaries. As an adult, you must be able to decide what things work for you and what doesn't. The restrictive beliefs, it's time to let them go and develop a new way of thinking that works for you. Beliefs should be unique and tailored to you because when you take on the ways of others, you won't experience your highest level of potential. It's a tragedy to accept a way of thinking and not trust it or have confidence in it. You only do it because it's all you know.

• **Spirituality**- No one should be able to tell you how to worship and appreciate the divine Creator. That decision should be left to you. Your relationship with the Creator is a unique experience. There are so many ways that you can connect with God but we have been trained to believe that the only way to connect with God is to go to church. This creates dependency on the church and it strips you of your power. Search deep within to find the things that connect you with the Creator. I love to go to the beach, and I love to be out in nature. Nature is God and God is nature. I also find the peace of God just by singing my favorite song. Taking a long walk on a hot sunny day can give you that spiritual connection to the Creator. Find yourself and you shall find God.

• **Thoughts**- Your thoughts are sacred because only you and God knows what goes on inside your mind. People can only know what you think if you reveal it to them. You and another individual can't think exactly alike. Your train of thought may be similar to another because it's either positive or negative. But, the thoughts that flow through your mind daily are unique.

• **Goals, Aspirations**- We all set different goals and aspirations. The ones you are interested in determine a part of your uniqueness. Your goals and aspirations are a part of your purpose and vision. We all have the same assignment as a whole, which is to come to Earth and solve problems, but how we do them is unique to us.

● **Your Creativity**- Your ability to create any type of work displays your uniqueness. If you are a chef, you will find out that the way you cook a dish would always be a little different from another chef. The only way it would be the same is if you follow their recipe. Your work would be easily identifiable if you allow your uniqueness and creativity to flow. When you create something using another person's pattern or their instructions you are not being unique or creative. You can do something that someone else already did, but make it yours by adding a different style to it. This is creativity. Creativity is about using critical thinking skills to help you develop new things. Creativity attracts people to you.

● **Attitude**- The way you approach circumstances determines your attitude. You can choose to be negative or positive. It is often called your mannerism. The way you approach things is very unique. You may not notice it, but it is.

These are some of the things that make you who you are and now is a good time to accept them, embrace them, and if changes need to be made, make changes. Never criticize yourself when you notice that there are some things that you need to change.

Regardless of your situation, when it comes to yourself, handle yourself with love.

Take a moment to look in the mirror and say, " I love you, I do".

You are Original

Uniqueness and originality work together. Uniqueness produces originality. God has given you the ability to create things that the world would want to see reproduced. You can invent or reinvent great things.

What are you so good at that when people need it they think of you? Why are they thinking of you? Are you the only person doing it? You're not the only person doing what you do. The reason they look for you is because they are captivated by how you do it. This is what makes you the best at what you do. People connect with others for a unique experience. When people see you as the best, then you know that you have especially touched the world.

"A true originator can never be copied, it would be too hard"

Prepare to be Lonely When You Decide to Embrace Who You Are

When you decide to stand out and be who you are you will meet opposition. It's hard for people who know themselves to find true friends because of jealousy and envy. This often leads to loneliness. It's better to have a few loyal friends than to have many friends and lose yourself in the process. Ordinary people have many friends, and those that are extraordinary have difficulties finding people they can trust.

This has nothing to do with you, it has to do with other people's insecurities. Never base your value and worth on how many friends and followers you have. It's better for someone to love you for who you are than to love you for who you're not. Besides, people that spend time alone are the most innovative ones. So, never sell yourself short to be approved by others. Develop self-assurance and not external assurance.

You are not Weird

When you decide not to conform to the things of the world, you are perceived as weird. The world is redefining what is normal, usual, or ordinary. What's 'weird' or 'unusual' is when you act out of character. To be weird is to hate yourself or compare yourself to another. Weird is not following your true purpose. Weird is not having that divine connection with the divine Creator. Weird is compromising your standards for the acceptance of others. Weird is accepting the 'new' normal even though you know it's not normal.

When you reject manipulation to 'fit in' you show people that you are a person of strength. This is confidence. You are not weird or strange, you're just unique!

IMPLEMENT BOUNDARIES in Your Life That Others Must Abide By

These boundaries are not for you, these boundaries are for the people you interact with. It is your responsibility to ensure that people respect you and respect the way you operate. If people don't agree with your morals and standards they have a right to, and you have a right to not associate with them. Set boundaries in your life that send a message to others that this is how I am, and if you can't respect me for who I am, we can't be friends or associates. When you set these standards, people will show you the respect that you deserve. Don't allow people to have access to you if they don't respect you. This is self-respect. Self-respect is recognizing your self-worth. When you know your worth, you make sure that people respect what you bring to the table. When you don't know your worth, and you don't tell others what you expect of them, and how they should treat you, they treat you how they want to treat you. Also, the results will not be favorable to you. Standing out from the crowd means sending an unapologetic message to others that says, "This is who I am, so accept it".

Don't Condemn Yourself for Being What God has Created You to Be

Do not condemn yourself or feel as if something is wrong with you because you choose to stand out and be different from the rest. Did you know that we can often be our top critic? Before people get the opportunity to judge you, how many times did you judge yourself? Guilt and shame are the two lowest emotions. So, we have been taught how to forgive others unlimitedly, but how often do you forgive yourself? How much luggage of pain lives inside your heart? Make a decision today to forgive yourself for past mistakes. Always show yourself acts of kindness and avoid cruel thoughts towards yourself. The Most High never wanted us to be perfect, but simply to just be good.

Being approved, loved, rewarded, appreciated, or recognized by others is not important as self-love.

There is no love, as powerful as self-love! Sherique Dill

Chapter Five
The Power of Meditation

"In the attitude of silence the soul finds the path in a clearer light, and what is elusive and deceptive resolves itself into crystal clearness. Our life is a long and arduous quest after Truth."
Mahatma Gandhi[1]

I STATED EARLIER, THAT we are body, mind, and spirit. This is the holy trinity within us. How many of you know that the mind carries the body? What does this mean? Well, whatever state the mind is in, it affects the body. If you're depressed, the body responds to this, if you're anxious, the body responds to this. The mind is the highest place within us because we can't operate if we can't rationalize or perceive things. This is where our understanding lies. So, as powerful as the spirit is, because it is the divine connection between you and the Creator, you still need the mind to perceive what the Creator is saying to you.

For this reason, we must take care of our mental state. Many people feed the body and take care of their physical appearance. They buy the best clothes and the best shoes. But, what are they doing to cultivate their minds? It doesn't matter how great your appearance is, how much money you have, how big your house is, or how many seminars you attend. If you don't have the skills and

1. http://en.wikipedia.org/wiki/Mohandas_Karamchand_Gandhi

abilities to nurture your mind it all means nothing. Here in this chapter, you will see why the mind is a terrible thing to waste.

The mind is responsible for your awareness of what is going on around you. Many call your mind your 'soul'. This is where you do your logical reasoning about your everyday life. All habits, behaviors, beliefs, morals, and every other thing that creates your personality begin within the mind. Before you were cognizant of who you were, your mind existed. The subconscious part of your mind makes up 80-90 percent of your mind. That means that most of the things you do today, you learned when you were a child. Many things were also learned from you being in your mother's womb.

The mind is very powerful because this is where your thoughts and ideas flow. Your thoughts determine your intellect. Your intellect or mental power plays an important role in how successful you will become in life and the quality of life you enjoy.

Soothe Your Mind Through Meditation

A good way to stay aware of what is happening in your mind is to meditate. Meditation is one way that you can connect to your higher self, and by extension, connect with The Most High. Today, life is so fast, and many of us don't have the time to slow down and do the things that matter. There is the television, the radio, social media, magazines, games, friends, cellphones, and so much more. Life is so fast today due to technology, that people have a problem sitting still for just ten minutes. They are constantly moving and busy. The distraction level is so high, and if you don't get control of your life you will be devoured. Technological advancements rob us of setting goals, critical thinking, organizing, being strategic, and personal power.

Meditation will help you to slow down and relax. It will help you to recognize your thoughts and your feelings. It can help you to heal from traumatic and painful events. Meditation is the route to nurturing your mind, and balancing your life.

When you meditate you are engaging in contemplation, reflection of thoughts, or in a mental exercise (concentration on one's breathing or repetition of a mantra) to reach a heightened level of spiritual awareness. You need to have time set out just to meditate. The best time to meditate is early in the morning upon rising because this is when the body is at its most hydrated state. Also, you want to command your day, by setting the tone for your day. This is a great time to make affirmations. The affirmations that you release into the atmosphere early in the morning, will control the rest of your day. Upon waking up, say your prayers of gratitude.

We can get so tied up with life that we don't have the time to properly plan what direction we want our lives to go in. Meditation is a good method that can be used to set goals. This is where you need to search deep inside yourself to determine what your talents and gifts are, and most of all what your purpose is in life. This time should be used to evaluate yourself, find out your weaknesses, your strengths, what makes you unique, what you are passionate about, and your character style. Your time should be spent on understanding what to adjust about yourself and how to increase your knowledge about life. Great revelations flow while you are in still mode. You will be surprised at how close your relationship can grow with The Creator just by being obedient and listening. Meditating is not about you making requests to the Universe, but simply just being silent, and listening. Use soothing calm music that helps you to listen to your thoughts.

Suitable Environments for Meditation

By now, it should be of no surprise to you that one of my favorite places to meditate is at the beach. When I visit the beach, awesome ideas flow. In such a peaceful setting I have the opportunity to contemplate on which goals I want to achieve in my life. People miscalculate the power of healing that nature can bring. Try it today, just go on the beach and sit somewhere directly in front of the water. It's amazing when the sea breeze blows upon you. The beautiful scenery of the beach introduces peace and thoughts of serenity. I would always carry a notepad and a pen because I knew that my mind would be at its highest level of awareness. While meditating at the beach, I was reminded of the 23rd Psalm of David. "He leads me beside quiet waters, He refreshes my soul". (NIV) This verse signifies the peacefulness of being beside still waters, and how it can restore your soul from brokenness or whatever you may need to be restored from.

An environment that is very popular with most people for meditation is inside their homes. You can sit upright on the floor, with scented candles around you, and make sure that there is no distraction. It must be a quiet place where no one can bother you. It is good to choose a familiar place. If there is a favorite place in your house that you normally use, stick to this atmosphere. Consistency is key in whatever we do. The reason why it's important to have the candles and scent is because it connects you to nature. The flames of the candle are the element of fire (nature). Also, good-smelling fragrances are commonly used to calm the mind. Whatever you choose, just know that whatever makes you happy, stick to it.

Breathing Techniques

We spoke about how technology is responsible for people not being able to calm down and relax. Think about it, how many times do you check your cell phone each day? Most people can't put their cell phones down, and this has eaten away people's ability to properly socialize. How many times have you gone to dinner with your family and found yourself on the phone, checking your social media profile? This is a challenge.

A good way to calm down and relax is to incorporate breathing techniques into your routine. Here is the breathing technique that I use:

- Sit upright in a very comfortable position

- You can play some meditation music to relax you a bit

- Take a deep breath ensuring that your stomach blows up like a balloon. Your stomach should move outwards on your inhale.

- Hold your breath for about 5 seconds

- Exhale slowly as your stomach collapses, or goes inwards.

- Repeat this step about 6 times

Another good technique that you can use while meditating and breathing, is the tapping technique. The tapping technique is tapping on certain parts of the body, pressure points, to relieve stress and tension. These points are the forehead, behind the neck, temples, nose, chin, chest, etc. While you're tapping you're talking to yourself and making affirmations. For example, I'm safe, I know I'm afraid right now, and I'm not sure where the fear comes from, but I have no reason to be afraid at this moment. I declare peace at this moment."

These exercises are extremely important if you need to clear anxiety and stress. When the body is anxious the oxygen levels drop because your breathing becomes more shallow and rapid. This means that you're not taking in enough oxygen in the body. When you lack proper oxygen the body is automatically stressed. Here are some benefits of doing breathing exercises:

➤ It helps you to stay calm and relax, lowering the dangers of the stress hormones cortisol on your body

➤ It lowers your heart rate

➤ It lowers your blood pressure levels

➤ It lowers panic and anxiety attacks

➤ It relaxes the muscles

➤ Improves sleep and fights insomnia

➤ When the blood is highly oxygenated it's hard for viruses and bacteria to grow in your body

➤ Maintain overall health

Many people don't have the time to sit still and do breathing exercises. Doing this is standing out and being different. Breathing and meditation combat indecisiveness and confusion. When you practice breathing techniques you'll also realize the demise of certain aches and pains in your body. Breathing is an excellent way to release a lot of toxins that we are faced with day to day due to the foods we eat, the water we drink, technology, lack of exercise, and much more.

THE BENEFITS OF MEDITATION

There are so many benefits that derive from meditation. The first benefit is that meditation is very relaxing. Why? Because the body has to be in still mode for meditation to be effective, it promotes relaxation. Then it builds internal energy or life force. It makes you aware of the things that matter in life, things such as love, compassion, kindness, and forgiveness. Another benefit is that it strengthens your concentration skill. When you become aware of how your mind works, you will be able to direct your focus on what you choose to focus and concentrate on. You can look at life more positively. Instead of dwelling on the negative things that can affect you, you can concentrate on the good aspect of life.

When you meditate, you will feel a difference in your body. Many of the health issues happening in the world today could have been easily prevented by meditation. It was said that people who meditate are usually happier. It helps you to sleep better because the mind is rejuvenated during meditation. This means that issues such as high blood pressure, depression, anxiety, fear, phobias, and anger are released because it promotes good mental and emotional balance. There are many different benefits of meditation when it comes to your personal life also. Meditation helps to develop good habits and good behaviors that can help an individual lead a more disciplined life.

Whether you are a busy person or not or whatever lifestyle you choose to live, the fact remains that the body needs its rest. There is something special about rejuvenation. When things are not going the way you would like them to, meditation can open up your mind and allow you to be more optimistic. It is said that when awareness rises, so does wisdom.

Sometimes we have those busy days when we have a lot of things to do. On these busy days, you can feel overwhelmed. You can feel your mind racing and then confusion sets in, or frustration. What I do when this happens is I say within my mind, "Peace be still", I also say, "Hush, we will be okay." What I am doing here is I am letting the subconscious mind know that we are safe, and that consciously I am standing strong.

Meditation Does not Belong to any Religion

Many people connect meditation to religion or cult activity. This is not true. Our ancestors have used meditation for thousands of years because of its benefits. You don't have to belong to a particular religion or cult to do this. Some religious groups may use it more in their daily routine, but this doesn't mean that the method belongs to them. Meditation is about spirituality, not religion. This is one of the keys to maintaining mental balance and staying in connection with the divine Creator. Therefore, use this method for your well-being regardless of your religious affiliation.

"To Know Thy Creator Is To Know Thyself" Sherique Dill

Chapter Six
Renew the Mind

Your mind is a battlefield. It is a battlefield because this is where you constantly fight good and evil. Or, it is where you decide what you will and will not do. The systems of this world are fighting for your mind. They want to be in control of this powerhouse. Whichever force you allow to take control of your mind and affect your way of thinking will dominate you. Your thoughts have a tremendous impact on your life because everything that exists, exists because of a thought that has been manifested into the physical realm. Thoughts breed emotions, and emotions breed thoughts. If you're allowing negative thoughts to flow through your mind, you will find yourself in a vicious cycle, not being able to control your life. Evaluate your actions. Are the things you engage in, you were programmed to do? Everywhere you turn people desire to brainwash you. The television, the ads and promotions, the financial institution, educational systems, the government, organizations, religious entities, and much more. This is why many companies pay big dollars on advertising and marketing because if they can program you through subliminal messages, they can get you to do what they want. These people have many tactics and schemes to control you. However, you must be more intelligent and not fall into these traps.

Many of us have been conditioned by work, parents, religion, school, and society. These systems have taught us from a tender age who we are, and how we should think. We were not encouraged to use our power and find out things for ourselves. We've been trained to follow what we've been told whether it is true or false. This is called psychological conditioning. It's being trained to value something that is not authentic to you, you only value it because it appears valuable to others.

"And do not be conformed to this world, but be transformed by the renewing of your mind, that you may prove what is that good and acceptable and perfect will of God." (Romans 12:2)NKJV

Standing out from the crowd and not fitting in, requires transformation. The steps to transformation are awareness, acknowledgment, acceptance, and action.

Renewing Your mind is Important

Renewing the mind is important because many things that we believed, no longer suit reality. Furthermore, they're limiting beliefs. When you become aware of them, remove them. How many things you wanted to do, you didn't because you believed you couldn't achieve them? These beliefs are not your own, someone embedded them there. This is why consistent transformation is necessary.

Mental slavery is more severe than physical slavery because people don't know that they are mental slaves. They're not aware that their behavior, thoughts, emotions, and actions are conditioned by others. Mental slaves can take care of themselves, but they're dependent on others. When you depend on someone else for life's necessities, you are not responsible.

Political Slavery

This is what politicians and government organizations do. They make you depend on them so that they can control you. They control you through economic oppression. They intentionally set laws and policies that are not beneficial to citizens. These laws and policies affect the cost of living. When the cost of living is high, people tend to seek refuge from politicians and governmental bodies. Politics is full of many tricks. Politicians need you to depend on them. When you depend on them they can continually manipulate you to vote for them so that they can maintain power. People that don't depend on politicians, rather, they make things happen for themselves, live more freely. Politicians want to be worshiped as demigods.

One of the simplest ways for you to make enemies is to be vocal about your political affiliation. Political slaves don't use their ability to see that while they display hatred and bitterness towards one another, the leaders who pretend to be at war are in harmony and unity. They are unified in creating wealth for themselves and their families. They don't have the nation's interest in their hearts. This is why when it comes to politics no matter how many times you change the government, all of them have the same agenda. They go into politics to make life harder for us, not better.

You can identify a political slave easily because they don't come out of the campaign mode, even after elections are over. They constantly fight with others that are not a part of their political party.

The manipulation of politics can turn mothers against daughters, fathers against sons, friends against friends, husbands against wives, and employers against employees. A political slave will say things like, "I am a die-hard", or "I will support this party until I die". They will even say "I do not care what they do; I support them because I like them". This type of action is not ignorant. If the party that you support does immoral things and does not benefit you, your children, your country, or the generations to come, why support them?

"We are going to emancipate ourselves from mental slavery because whilst others might free the body, none but ourselves can free the mind." Marcus Garvey

Only you can free yourself from mental slavery. Freedom is having the ability to make your own decisions and choices. Freedom is being accountable for yourself. This is personal power. Freedom is having the opportunity to create wealth for you and your family. When it comes to my needs and wants, I rely on inner strength, inner capabilities, and my great divine mind.

Your Mind is Like a Filing Cabinet

Picture the responsibility of a filing clerk. Filing clerks create files and store them. Your mind is like a filing cabinet. The files represent thoughts and emotions from your experiences. Every thought you have produces a feeling or emotion. Each time you feel or experience something, it is stored in your mind.

Sometimes, mistakes are made. Some documents are stored in the wrong file. Also, some experiences are new and instead of creating a new file, that experience is placed in an existing file. So the things that you believe are dangerous might not be. For example, Susan was engaged in a relationship. In this relationship, she discovered that her partner was unfaithful. This doesn't make her feel good. For many months she was distraught. Her heart was broken. Susan feels now that no matter how good the man may appear to be, he can't be trusted. One day she met a man. Things were going great, but all of a sudden those previous emotions started flowing in. She started to think, "I don't know if I can trust this guy, I don't want to get my heart broken again." Instead of creating a new file, she judges her partner based on her previous experiences.

Renewing the Mind is a Lifelong Habit

The process of transforming your mind doesn't happen overnight. This is not a skill that people are born with. Having the ability to recognize your toxic mindset and make changes, is a skill learned over a while. It is something that gets better by practicing and consistency.

Some Ways That You Can Break Mental Slavery:

- **Challenge your way of thinking-** If you have a train of thought that you're not comfortable with, challenge it. It's important to revisit beliefs and old ways of doing things that don't work well for you. Many people get stuck in their comfort zones. They know that the things they consistently do aren't working, but they repeat them. This is insanity.

- **Pay Attention to Your Thoughts-** The best way to take control of your mindset is to monitor your thoughts. Don't allow negative thoughts to constantly flow and dominate your mind. When negative thoughts flow, recognize them, and how it makes you feel. You can interrupt these destructive thoughts by rebuking them and not believing them. Clear them out of your mind by using your breathing techniques and making affirmations. Soon you will realize the thoughts diminish. So, the key is to replace negative thoughts with positive thoughts.

- **Be Confident When Making Decisions-**You will not know if you're right or wrong until you decide to step out and do it. It's important to know that you will not always be right. Whatever the outcome, be confident with your decisions. Feeling doubtful when making a decision will cause you to procrastinate. Researching your steps and carefully planning, will help you to feel less anxious with your goals and be more confident with your decisions. Also, never make haste decisions. Second-guessing your decisions due to intuition doesn't prove that you're doubtful, it could be a sign of wanting to be responsible and accountable for your actions. Being able to make decisions and stand by them no matter what is a trait of a good leader and it depicts a person with an unwavering mindset.

• **Knowing Your Emotional Triggers**-Understanding what triggers you is crucial to being mentally free. All of us wrestle with some trauma or painful experience. Knowing what triggers you is important because it avoids being an emotional wreck. This is emotional intelligence. Emotional intelligence is being able to control how you respond to a situation. When you respond to a situation in a way that you regret later, your emotions were hijacked by someone or something. Awareness helps you to identify what is going on so that you can find the proper tools to heal and be restored. For example, if drinking alcohol is a weakness that you have, then being around people that drink alcohol would be a trigger. Or going to a party with lots of alcohol could produce destructive results for you. So avoiding such situations or developing the strength to not participate, is a tool or a skill.

• **Be Logical and Rational**- Amateurs make decisions while highly emotional. When you're highly emotional, you tend to think more from the right side of your brain. The right side of your brain is creative, imaginative, and emotional. The left side of your brain is logical, rational, and analytical. To avoid actions that you'll later regret, balance your emotions with logic. This means learning how to activate your left brain when trying to solve a problem. The left brain is designed to solve problems. To activate your left brain when confronted with a problem, take a few deep breaths. Then, give yourself some time to think before you act. Taking deep breaths brings down the emotions and allows your logical thoughts from your left brain to flow. Due to the creativity of the right brain, you tend to hear things that weren't said, or perceive things in the wrong way: imaginations. So, knowing when to use each side of the brain is crucial. The right brain is perfect to use when you have a new idea because it allows you to see the end from the beginning. It allows your creativity to flow from the endless possibilities of your imagination.

- **Practice Gratitude**- It's hard to be negative and not operate in your divine true self when you feel so blessed. Being grateful helps you to vibrate at a high frequency. People that complain a lot find themselves vibrating at low frequencies often. When your frequency is high you will accomplish more and set a clearer direction for your life. You will often experience abundance and prosperity because you attract it to you through gratitude. When you aren't thankful, and you always complain instead of being responsible, you will live life in scarcity.

- **Act on Your Advice**- Some people give good advice but they don't set an example. The same good advice that you give to other people, follow them yourself.

Otherwise, it is hypocrisy. Trust yourself the same way you trust a friend, and reward yourself the same way you reward others. When you take your advice it shows that you value yourself and you trust yourself.

A Cage Called Job

Let's elaborate on why jobs are slavery tools. You don't control two valuable assets when you have a job: time and money. There is very little leverage. You have to work one hour to be paid one hour. If you don't go to work, you won't be paid. Jobs were designed to keep the wealth in the hands of the rich. My objective here is not to bash jobs, because jobs are good starting points. However, it's important to know that it's very challenging to become wealthy at a job. Your money is limited by your employer. So, your lifestyle is controlled, and they pay you just enough to be 'Just Over Broke'. People can't enjoy themselves with the salary that they make because it's not enough to live, just survive. You can't transfer your job to your kids or grandkids like a business because it doesn't belong to you. Reality is, you're building someone else's dream.

If you choose a job that isn't aligned with your purpose or passion, you find yourself just working for a check. This is when it becomes degrading and can lower your self-esteem.

Standing out from the crowd means controlling your destiny by mastering your time and money. Jim Rohn says, "Work harder on yourself than you do at your job."

Religion can also be a Condition of a Mental Slave

Religion is very powerful. Religion plays a very significant role when it comes to your beliefs and your code of conduct. Due to religion being the basis of people's beliefs and standards, it's a delicate topic. We should respect the rights of others and allow people to be free to believe what is fundamental to them. Religion is only a cultural expression of what we think The Most High is. This is why so many religions exist. Belief is not facts. We can only believe and hope for things that we haven't experienced. However, there are some good things the religious communities have done.

The foundation of religion is control. Religion is not spirituality. When your routine of serving the Creator is dictated to you by groups and organizations, this is religion. When they develop a set of rules that you must abide by if you wish

to be a part of their religious organization you're being controlled. Spirituality is connecting with the Creator in any way you choose. Since having a relationship with The Most High is personal, no one can dictate to you how it should be done. For example, some organizations claim that the correct way to worship God is to kneel, and some organizations say that you should stand and close your eyes. Some religious organizations create the misconception that for you to truly worship The Creator you must come to church. This is a big misconception, and it drives the false narrative that you can only experience the power of God when listening to the pastor, or being in the church building.

Whatever religion or form of spirituality works for you, accept it into your life. If it doesn't benefit you or make your life better, why follow it?

In addition, some religions breed undisciplined behavior. They lead people to believe that they are saved by grace no matter what they do. They then cause their followers to feel as if they're not responsible for their actions and behaviors. It wasn't them who made the bad decision, it was the devil.

Many religious groups use religion to gain wealth. They care more about prosperity than making a positive impact on the lives of others. Their most famous quote is 'Will a man rob God, he does it in his tithes and offering." I believe in the law of giving. I believe that when you give not under compulsion because The Creator loves a cheerful giver, blessings will flow your way. But religion has brainwashed people to think that you must bring your tithes and offerings to the church. It doesn't count if you help a mother or father in need with your offerings, because that belongs to God, and God is in the church. This type of religion is manipulation. As they become richer, you, the religious slave, become poorer.

'Religious Slaves' often believe whatever their pastor/leader says to them without searching for the truth themselves. Many people fall into this trap because they don't comprehend that God is an energy. They often believe the misconception of God or The Creator being a person. Many have been trained to pray to the Heavenly Father alone, leaving out the blessed mother. The Creator cannot just be a father since we're made in the image of God. There must also be a motherly side of God to represent the image of the blessed female species on earth. If not, then whose image is the women made in?

You will be able to identify a religious slave because they only read the Bible. When it comes to other books, they declare they don't like to read. They are afraid to ask questions or challenge their religious masters because they fear they would be called 'the devil' or 'a demon'. This is what religion does to people. It tells people what to eat, what to drink, what to wear, what to believe, how to act, how you should fix your hair and the list goes on.

Religion has brainwashed its audience into thinking that life is only about serving God. That is why the world lacks the spirit of love towards one another, which the Messiah often spoke about. It has created people that have become emotionless, lifeless, and dull. No wonder why a lot of the 'Religious Slaves' are weary and tired of life, and they pray to die so that they can go to Heaven.

I often wonder why there aren't any inspirational or religious singers that sing about the love between a husband and a wife or a man and a woman. What a beautiful thing it would be to have positive people positively singing love songs. Instead, singers of negative music take pleasure in singing the kind of love songs that promote promiscuous acts. Not only are they promoting negative behaviors, but the lyrics are demonic and destructive. Religious singers probably do not want to sing love songs because they will be labeled 'singers of that devil music'.

The reality is that the systems of this world are against you. They compete for your soul. Will you let them have it? Are you a sheep or a lion? Sheep don't do anything but follow their shepherd.

The majority of the people that exist are followers and easily manipulated. Are you standing out from this crowd? With all of the topics that we have discussed so far, you should be in good standing. Remove all of the lies from your belief system and live in your truth! You can always determine the truth because it shall make you free.

Chapter Seven
Loyalty to Self

Today, in modern times, it's hard to find loyal friends, partners, associates, and family members. Due to high levels of trauma since childhood, people are cautious about who they trust. Also, some people find out quickly that they can be loyal and committed to others, but people are not loyal or committed to them. What do you do when you show loyalty to others but they don't show loyalty to you? The truth is that you can't command people on how they should love you or commit to you. People act based on what they know, and what they have been taught. So what could you do? The way you wish for people to be loyal, faithful, and committed to you, you could put that same energy into yourself. When was the last time you looked in the mirror, and said, "I love you?" What emotions are you experiencing? Do you think you're a success or a failure?

Being loyal to schedules is about creating a routine for your life. Your life should operate in order or within a system. This is a consistent system. You are recurrent with your actions and behavior.

Stay Loyal to Your Schedules and Appointments

Here are some ways that you can be loyal to yourself:

1. Show commitment to your schedules and

      appointments
2. Don't be your biggest critic
3. Be honest about your emotions and feelings
4. Achieve your goals
5. Believe in yourself
6. Be kind to yourself
7. Consistently make changes when they need to be made
8. Get feedback from people that respect you
9. Don't compromise your character
10. Save yourself from regrets

When you set dates and deadlines, honor them. This is a way of respecting yourself. Many people don't achieve goals because of disloyalty. If you don't trust yourself by staying committed and faithful to the things you deem important, who should trust you? Professional people don't connect with people who are not trustworthy. Stay loyal to your schedules by setting reminders on calendars or phone apps. Loyalty is a part of self-love. Give yourself the support and love you hoped to get from others.

Don't Compromise Your Character

You need to be resolute with yourself and others about the things you will and will not do. When you have a strong character, people know without having to ask what you will not do. Your character should stand out. When you engage in things that are not a part of your character you're compromising. You compromise your character when you go against your beliefs and standards for short-lived benefits. When you have a weak character, others can manipulate you to act out of your ordinary self. Allow your light to be different when you're present. Avoid trading your soul and what makes you who you are to please others.

Get Feedback From People That Respect You

We have been conditioned to think that feedback is bad. So, people dislike feedback. As humans, we don't like to hear about our wrongs or weak areas. We don't like when people reveal areas in our lives that need transformation. Feedback is a great thing. Whether you like the messenger or not, always pay attention to the message. Listen to what is said. If you can find some truth in what is being said, implement it. You don't control where feedback comes from. However, you can control how you respond to it.

Feedback is helpful information that is given about a person, product, or service for improvement and development. This is what good constructive feedback is.

Some people claim to give feedback but it's negative criticism. How do you know negative criticism? After the feedback your self-confidence is low and your energy is drained. The person giving the feedback pointed out all your weaknesses but never offered a solution. You want to avoid these types of people. As I said, you can't control the message or the messenger, but you can control your emotions and your actions. No one knows you better than you. You know the truth about yourself. If the feedback is true, reject denial. Accept the fact that you need to improve in those areas. If the feedback is false and it seeks to lower your self-confidence, be calm, and act maturely. Don't allow the feedback to take root in your subconscious mind.

People that respect you and want to see you grow will give you good feedback. They will always suggest a better alternative. This alternative will improve and enhance your life.

Consistently Make Changes

As things are revealed to you and you acknowledge and accept that there are some areas in your life where you need change, make the changes. As you set goals for your life, consistently review your action steps to see what is working for you. Keep the steps that bring you closer to your achievements. Delete steps that have low results. This should be constant. For example, if you realize that you procrastinate frequently when it comes to achieving something, observe why. Why do you procrastinate and what can you do to change this habit? What can you do to be a better decision-maker and avoid wrestling with indecisiveness? What changes can you implement that will help you to be a greater planner? Are you looking for skills that are needed for your job? When can you enroll yourself in a seminar that will help you with this?

Standing out from the crowd means rejecting mediocrity and being phenomenal.

Avoid Regrets

The saddest thing that could happen to someone, is to be tormented with regrets. Regrets are opportunities that came your way but you didn't seize them. These are the shoulda, coulda, and if I only had done this. Or, maybe you went after some opportunities but you made some decisions that were not in your best interest. However, all regrets are not bad. Regrets remind us how important it is to cautiously think about decisions and choices. Regrets help us to learn ourselves better and what we truly desire for ourselves.

Most opportunities don't come back to you the same way. So when you notice an opportunity, act swiftly. It would be very sad to lay on your deathbed, not able to leave this world in peace because there are so many things that you procrastinated with. You know you could do it, and you didn't.

Procrastinators delay or put off things that are good for them.

In the book The Richest Man in Babylon, it says, " Opportunity is a haughty goddess who wastes no time with those who are unprepared." Also, it says, " A procrastinator accepts no opportunity when she comes. He awaits. He says I have much business right now. Bye and bye I talk to you. Opportunity, she will not wait for such a slow fellow. She thinks if a man desires to be lucky he will step quickly. Any man who does not stop quickly when the opportunity comes is a big procrastinator".

So as you can see from the wisdom that lies in this book, good luck flees from procrastinators.

Reasons why People Don't Remain Loyal to Their Schedules:

1. They tend to forget them
2. Procrastination
3. Indecisiveness
4. Distractions
5. Lack of passion
6. Self-doubt

7. Fear of failure or success
8. Lack of commitment

When you implement self-discipline into your lifestyle, you will stand out far from the crowd. This takes endurance and a great amount of sacrifice. Most people that exist don't have what it takes to live a disciplined life. You have the opportunity to separate yourself. Will you procrastinate? Or choose to make changes now.

Chapter Eight
No Competition

―――――

As you begin to know yourself your outlook on competition will change. We were not created to compete with one another. The spirit of competition interrupts unity. Unity is powerful and beautiful. The competitive spirit interrupts unity because instead of you seeing the opportunity for having a good friendship you will be busy devising plans to defeat others. Competition breeds hate, jealousy, covetousness, wickedness, and so many other negative emotions. There would be no need for competition if people truly know themselves. When you know yourself it's hard to envy others. Not only is it profitable to know oneself, but also to understand others. All of us need to survive on this planet and no one is better than the next. Envy is an excuse for not taking responsibility for your own life.

When you maximize the gifts and talents that you have, no one is your competition. No two people are alike. Instead of worrying about other people having more skills or abilities than you, focus more on your craft. Whatever area you exert energy in, it grows. If you focus on the success of others, you will continue to see them outperform you. If you focus on yourself, you recognize growth and development.

I have another quote from one of my favorite books to read, The Richest Man in Babylon says, "The more wisdom we know, the more we may earn. That man who seeks to learn more of his craft shall be richly rewarded. I urge all men to be in the front rank of progress and not to stand still, lest they be left behind."

Connect with people that share the same interest as you rather than compete with them. Your strength is someone's weakness and your weakness is someone's strength. This is the mastermind group that we previously spoke about. So, I don't desire to compete with others, I respect the talent and gift that they have, understanding that all of us have the same mandate but will accomplish it differently or uniquely.

Good Competition

Competing with others occasionally is good if it helps you to advance. Some people find it fun to compete with friends, classmates, and teammates. If competing with others causes you emotional distress, and low self-esteem, it is unhealthy.

If you choose to compete, allow the competition to motivate you and draw you closer to your goals. It's easy to compete with others. Stand out from the crowd and compete with yourself. You are your only match. If you must have real competition, allow your future to compete with your past. In the end, you'll want the future to win.

Comparing yourself to others is self-cruelty. You have no clue what experiences people had to endure to achieve what they have. This leads to a life of self-judgment and self-criticism. This is not true success. This is why you should not covet. Covet means to lust after or have a strong desire for what other people have. This is dangerous because you end up living a lie. You create a life that is pleasing to others, but it brings you no true happiness. Races are not for the swiftest but those that can endure to the end, and the race doesn't have to be against anybody but yourself.

Here are some ways that you can refocus your energy on the competition:

- **Appreciate the abilities of Others**- When you become too competitive based you end up missing the efforts of others

- **Learn From Teamwork**- Selfishness causes you to lose out. When you focus on becoming the best, you miss out on quality relationships. When you focus more on creating good quality relationships you'll find yourself learning more, because we learn from others. Do you know that good relationships are a form of wealth?

- **Don't Sabotage Others**- It's easy to hurt other people when you see them as your competition. True success is not gained through the misery of other people. Some people will do anything to win. Even if it means doing ungodly things to cause pain and suffering. When you remove the negative energy of competing, you clear yourself of committing unjust acts.

- **There Will Always be Someone That Challenges' You**- If your goal is to always be the best by taking down your competition, you'll always be in the rat race. Instead, celebrate small progress and improvements. Become someone that you love being. Stick to things that you're good at, to avoid frustrations, disappointments, and self-criticism. Nothing is a mistake, your gifts and talents are yours for a reason. Be grateful for what you have.

Chapter Nine
Becoming a Master of Your Trade

I know you've heard the term "Jack of all trades, Master of none". The world is changing rapidly with artificial intelligence. Many of the things that worked, no longer work. With artificial intelligence, many skills will become extinct. As we look around the world today, there is evidence of this. The banking system globally is quickly erasing certain services because they rely on the robotic system. Banks don't need tellers at the counters anymore, they have reverted to ATMs. We can deposit cheques at the ATM, deposit money to our savings, and withdraw. Also, funds are available instantly, just like how it was with a teller inside the bank. Today, you don't have to go inside the bank, you can seek information from your online banking account.

Do you remember Kodak? The company that created cameras? Well, smartphones have replaced them. People can take beautiful pictures right from their phones. They don't need a photographer. When you go to the food stores, kiosks are available. These kiosks replaced the cashiers. People can scan their groceries and pay with their credit or debit cards, without a cashier's assistance. How do you like these 24-hour online chat services? These designed robots are replacing receptionists and customer service agents. Remember those days when you had to look for dictionaries to ensure that a word was correct when typing a letter? Today we have Grammarly and other sites that edit documents for you. So, professional editors are also being replaced. Plans for home building are now being designed virtually. There is no need for old articheat drawings.

So, people must move with this change. There are so many opportunities today, and learning something new and exciting is becoming easier each day. Skills and education no longer have to be learned at institutions or schools. People are simply learning from blogs on the internet, videos, and all kinds of different methods. Youtube has become the go-to site to learn new skills. Artificial intelligence is replacing many jobs and putting a lot of people out of work.

We are undoubtedly living in a very unsecured world, which is probably why people are afraid to branch out and pursue their dreams and visions. Nothing seems secure anymore and people do not feel safe. This is why there is a high demand for jobs that can offer security; such as government jobs and so forth; people want security.

It's good to be able to multitask because you don't know when you will have to rely on a certain skill. However, with artificial intelligence, one must be more strategic than ever. We must carefully plan so that our skills don't become extinct. Repetitive skills can be replaced with artificial intelligence. Skills that are creative and unique are difficult to replace.

For example, as of today, no robot can deal with human emotions. Artificial intelligence is a human being programming a machine. They can only put intelligence into the robot from the knowledge they have. So, these machines can never know everything, and they don't understand human emotion. Since all of us are different and unique, we have a long way to go to be able to find a robot that can truly understand the ups and downs of our emotions and feelings.

To survive this powerful technological change, one must master themselves. One must begin to focus on what they're naturally good at, and capitalize on it. One must allow their creativity. Being a 'Jack of all Trades' is stressful. It means that you have to constantly keep up with various fields. It requires great sacrifice in your personal life, and your family life and is also very time-consuming. You can become burned out very quickly if you are not careful. This is so because when you are learning more than one field, your time has to be divided into all of them and because your time is divided it is very hard to master even one. Your focus and concentration are also divided and less potent. Also, to reach the level of expertise you must perform the task habitually. If you're a multi-tasker, many skills will be abandoned. It's just too much energy trying to keep out. Focus on specialization. You must realize that you cannot go after every opportunity that is introduced, it is impossible to learn everything and be productive.

Mastering requires discipline, focus, and direct attention. When you focus on mastering yourself, you discover valuable skills. What you want is to become an expert in your gifted area. There is no artificial intelligence that can outperform a person that lives a life of purpose. A person that effortlessly serves humanity is irreplaceable. One of the most powerful things about a human being is our ability to change. You can have a rough five years, make a change, and have a successful five years. We can change what we don't like.

People will have to learn how to truly serve others to survive. I would rather be served by a human than a robot. Humans can offer emotional support. Humans have intelligence from experience. Also, we have intuition. Intuition is spiritual.

So what are some creative abilities that are difficult to replace:

1. Musical and singing abilities
2. Writing creative books
3. Social work and Mentorship
4. Coaching
5. Art/Paintings
6. Nursing/ Health jobs
7. Human Resources

So from all of the things that we have discussed so far, it should be clear to you, the reason we need to focus on improving ourselves to avoid extinction. Mastering yourself is to have control over yourself. It means to not be a person easily swayed by his or her emotions. It means to do what you must despite your feelings. It means waking up every morning declaring that you will have a great day, no matter what. Mastering yourself is to live a life that is organized and properly planned. This is operating in your higher self. When you have The Most High on your side, nothing shall defeat you. You are never alone, there is help. You can always get help from the Universe and your ancestors. But, be prepared, and disciplined. You must do the work. To expect great things, but never do great things is insanity.

Chapter Ten
Opinion and Feedback

Organizations exist today that don't allow you to be who you are. Being who you are includes the right to express your opinions and feedback on matters. Today, stronger trends exist, where if you don't follow the status quo, you are called names or placed into groups. They put labels on individuals or certain groups that don't fit in. Some of these names are homophobic, bourgeoisie, capitalist, unvaccinated, xenophobic, and more. Many of these terms are used as bullying tactics. Governments and certain organizations want to maintain control. They don't want us to have the right to make our own decisions. They somehow feel as if they can make better decisions for us. They seek to decide where you live, what you eat, your income, where you can travel or work, what happens with your children, and more.

The labels are bullying tactics because the people that create them are hoping that it stops you from speaking out or believing what you believe due to the fear of being associated with a name or label. What has happened to the right or freedom to express your opinions or beliefs? When you're not encouraged to express yourself you're in a dictator environment. This is manipulation. No matter what your view is, you have the right to say how you feel and why. The moment this changes you've lost your right to freedom. It's not about who is right or wrong. Opinions are just that. It doesn't have to be facts. However, it's about having the maturity as a people to hear opposing views and be okay with that. What is offensive is when people believe what they believe and try to force their beliefs on you. When you show signs of not being interested in their beliefs, they call you names and become bullies. Bullies don't only exist in schools, there are bullies in governments, politics, law, organizations, and societies. People or systems are fighting to control your soul every day. They are programmers. Many of these programmers are found right on television and social media sites.

You know that they're bullying you because after you give your opinion or feedback on a particular matter you get a sense of regret and a feeling of wanting to withdraw because of people's reaction.

As long as you're being respectful with expressing yourself, respect should be given back to you. Therefore, for freedom and to maintain certain rights, and to fight against oppression, one must be strong. Should we continue to equip people with power that uses their power against us and torment us? This is a fight that must be fought collectively. This is the same with friends and families. Should you continue to surround yourself with people that don't honor how you feel? Many people have been friends for years and have yet to reveal their true selves. They keep their true feelings inside just to be loved and accepted. This is hypocrisy. This is acting, or putting on a mask. When you're alone you finally take off your mask. Surround yourself with people that value your abilities and accept who you are.

Your thoughts, beliefs, and opinions are unique to you. Both people could have been raised in the same house with the same parents, and still have a different experience. How we perceive things are also unique to us. Being robbed of this is like being a robot or someone's subject. It's slavery. Life becomes meaningless. I have no intention to join organizations that plan to put a bridle on my mouth. Or make me feel as if I have to follow their rules, and I don't get to choose. The Most High does not desire this for us. We are here to get the most out of our experience on this planet and we are the masters of our destiny.

Therefore, choose your path. This requires sacrifice and great strength. But freedom is worth fighting for. You will also have to be very careful with what and who you allow to program you. It's important to watch and listen to things that are in alignment with your standards, morals, and principles. People have become so fearful, that they seek others for guidance, other than their power. They have accepted the 'new norm', and feel as if there is nothing that can be done to fix things. However, nothing is new under the sun. We've been through this before where we faced people that were destructive and hateful towards humanity. There will be a time when we shall overcome it again. Listen to true things, of good report, peaceful, praiseworthy, and wise. Recognize programs that seek to bully and downplay who you are, and your right to choose.

Chapter Eleven
Too Great to Fit In

You will always know when you are on the right track because you will suffer persecution. People that are afraid to stand up for themselves, would compromise their beliefs and standards to please others. When you have a strong character, loneliness is common. You will not be popular or seen as a sociable person. This can make you question yourself. Sometimes you might think, "What am I doing wrong?", or, "What's wrong with me? Nothing is wrong with you. Wickedness is often exalted and those that do good deeds are often scorned. The fact that you experience persecution shows that you are doing something right. As a person living in the light, and having the ability to create effective change, this is reality. Do not mind those people who can 'fit in' no matter where they go. The question is, "What do they compromise that allows them to fit it?" You should never feel pressured to fit in or conform to the will, beliefs, behaviors, or opinions of others. I would rather be lonely if being lonely means I will get to be who I am. Conforming is a sign of weakness.

All of us have diverse needs, and they're very crucial to us. If these needs are not met, it affects our behavior and the things that we do. Some needs are:

- The need to be accepted and approved

- The need to be loved

- The need to be recognized

- The need to feel safe and secure

- The need for financial security

- The need to feel respected

- The need to be a part of a team

- The need to be in a relationship

Unmet needs often stem from childhood. As children, we need love, attention, and protection. As children, if our needs are not met, we still carry the desire to have them met into adulthood. As adults, we consistently search for those needs to be met by others. Those who have the need to be accepted and approved by others will be in jeopardy of wanting to fit in. This causes people to go to extreme levels to get what they need. Why do people often care about the approval of others? Many people don't feel good about themselves if they can't hear good things about themselves from others. This is why self-motivation is key. Self-motivation is a stage of internal reassurance. Internal reassurance is the ability to trust the divine power within you. It is the ability to validate yourself without criticism. You need to have the ability to motivate yourself when no one else is in your corner. When you often seek the opinion of others about yourself, you're looking for validation. You should be your cheerleader or your biggest fan.

Getting feedback from others now and then is a good thing. Sometimes we need to hear other people's perceptions of us so that we can improve. But, their opinions ought not to be the foundation of your value and your worth. This is what you call external reassurance.

Self-doubt will push you to lower your standards to 'fit in'. Self-doubt is the reason behind a lot of anxiety and depression.

Don't Crave Friends

If choosing not to conform means that you will lose friends and be left alone by many, then so be it; it is better to have one true friend than have ten friends who don't have your best interest at heart. The fewer friends you have the less drama you will have in your life. Having a 'friend' requires trust, and the truth is that true friends don't come by easily. Associates do not require trust and you can have as many as you want, but be careful of who you call your friend (the ones you trust) because your trust can be easily betrayed. If you need people around you constantly, be prepared for a very troublesome life.

If you study most successful people, you will find that they do not have many friends. They have a lot of associates or acquaintances that they use as gateways to success, but they do not allow just anyone to have access to their personal space. Too many close friendships (with the wrong type of people) can be distracting and destructive. Being great requires a lot of personal and free time alone.

True friends don't require you to conform to their way of life. True friends accept and love you for who you are and admire you for your strength; after all, it was your uniqueness that attracted them to you in the first place. True friends will value you the same way you value them. Try to avoid those who can call on you when they are in need but when you are in need they are nowhere to be found. Or they always have an excuse why they can't be there. If you have those types of friends you certainly do not need enemies.

Develop Strategies and Take Action

It's natural to doubt yourself when you don't have a strategy or a plan. A good way to overcome self-doubt is talking to yourself out loud: Making affirmations. Say empowering things to yourself and soothe yourself when your mind seems weak. It's important to know that all of us are challenged with emotional triggers from childhood experiences. The key is to know your triggers and overcome them. The need for approval, love, and attention as a child is not part of your reality as an adult. Once you love yourself, give attention to yourself, and approve of yourself, this is what matters. No one has to believe in you but: you. The sooner you accept this, the greater your life will become. You are too great to 'fit in'.

All About Me

Sherique Dill was born in New Providence, Bahamas. She has three beautiful children. Dill loves to spend time with her family and she honors being a mother and a wife.

Professionally, Dill has 20 years of experience working as a Chief officer. In her career path, she has worked in payrolls, expenditure, human resources, and customer service.

Dill published her first book in 2014, "Created To Stand Out Not Fit In." In 2016, she published "A Cage Called Job."

Another book published recently by Dill is Becoming A Master of Self, published in 2021.

Sherique Dill is also an inspirational coach and online course creator. She loves to travel, read books, explore nature, and sing. Dill's foundation is spirituality. Her spiritual upbringing and beliefs are the foundation of her values, standards, and philosophies.

Other Books by Author Sherique Dill

Becoming a Master of Self

A Cage Called Job

A Beginner's Guide to Generational Wealth

Don't miss out!

Visit the website below and you can sign up to receive emails whenever Sherique Dill publishes a new book. There's no charge and no obligation.

https://books2read.com/r/B-A-FJHZ-SZMLC

BOOKS 2 READ

Connecting independent readers to independent writers.